Darcy Devlin
and the Mystery Boy

Story by Chris Bell

Illustrations by Vasja Koman

Rigby PM Plus Chapter Books
part of the Rigby PM Program
Sapphire Level

Harcourt Achieve Inc.
10801 N. MoPac Expressway
Building #3
Austin, TX 78759
www.harcourtachieve.com

10 9 8 7 6
07 06

Printed in China by 1010 Printing International Ltd

Darcy Devlin and the Mystery Boy
ISBN 0 75786 928 9

For my Mom and Dad with love and thanks

Contents

Chapter One

Something to Hide

"What's he up to?" Darcy wondered aloud as he stepped back into a better position. Concealed behind the bus shelter, he could watch the boy's strange behavior without being observed himself.

Darcy Devlin had always wanted to be a private investigator. He considered himself an amateur sleuth already. After all, who had solved the case of the disappearing mailboxes on Clyde Street?

He always kept his eyes and ears open and his notebook handy, just in case something strange caught his eye — like now.

He might not have even noticed the boy huddled at the end of the alley except for two things. One, the boy wore an electric blue cap, just like the one Darcy had been eyeing in the sports store window, and two, he acted weird.

All week Darcy watched him standing in the alley, looking right and left, as if to check if anyone was watching him. Then he'd step onto the street with a superior strut as if he didn't care who saw him.

Very suspicious, thought Darcy.

5

At first Darcy had studied the boy only with curiosity. He'd appeared lost. But then he'd turned up in the same place again the next day and the day after — with the same strange behavior! Coincidence?

Every now and then, the boy would glance up and down the street, and it was the look in his eyes that fascinated Darcy and kept him watching. Huge and dark, the boy's eyes reflected fear, reminding Darcy of a skittish colt ready to bolt at the first sign of danger.

Every day before school, Darcy had watched in frustration, unable to follow. But today was Saturday and he was going to find out what the boy was up to — even if he had to follow him all day.

The boy strolled slowly along, occasionally stopping to stare into a storefront. When he looked back up the street, Darcy ducked behind a lamppost.

When he passed Costa's Barbershop, Costa called out to him. "You ready for another haircut, Tai?" and he laughed heartily.

The boy gave a small smile. "Not yet, Costa!" he exclaimed, quickening his pace.

Aha! thought Darcy. His first breakthrough. A name! Tai.

Darcy quickly scribbled in his notebook.

7

Tai slouched beside a fruit stand to watch the passing shoppers, who took no notice of him.

But Darcy noticed. He saw Tai pick up a ripe, juicy apple and roll it in his hand.

"Buy it or drop it," barked the owner.

Tai sighed and replaced the apple. Suddenly a passing jogger jolted the cart sending apples, pears, and tomatoes rolling away down the sidewalk.

In a blink, Tai snatched up a wayward apple and slipped it into his pocket. He did it so swiftly that Darcy wondered if he had seen it at all.

Tai hurried back up the street and ducked into a doorway. He chomped into the apple as though he hadn't eaten for a week, then glanced up and caught Darcy's eye.

Red-faced, Darcy looked away. Was the boy homeless? Was he a runaway? So many questions. Well, he decided, the best way to get answers was to ask questions.

Darcy started innocently. "That was a lucky save, that apple."

Those dark eyes darted up at him before the boy glanced quickly each way, as if searching for an escape. He dodged past Darcy and broke into a run.

"Hey, I didn't mean anything," yelled Darcy, sprinting after him. "Come back!" But by the time he turned into the alley, the boy was gone.

Overhead, a seagull screeched and Darcy squinted up in time to see the gull dive to the sidewalk to peck at a crust of bread. But the seagull's swoop wasn't what held his eye.

On the second story, above the row of stores, he caught a flash of electric blue behind the window pane. He was just in time to catch a fleeting glimpse of Tai before a snowy curtain dropped back into place.

Chapter Two
Gathering Evidence

Later, when the town clock gonged, Darcy noted in his book: *1:00 P.M. No sign of Tai.*

He paced the storefronts and was just about to give up when he spotted the familiar patch of blue inside the electrical store. Tai, busily watching television, didn't notice the manager stride over. Seeing the manager's angry frown, Darcy could guess that Tai was not welcome in the store.

He asked himself, why does Tai need to watch television here? Doesn't he have a set at home? Does he have a home? Darcy flipped open his notebook.

Darcy looked up and scooted after Tai as he headed for the street, but before he could catch up, a woman from the bakery called, "Hey, Tai. Look what I've got for you."

Tai stopped and turned around, smiling shyly, and the woman handed him a white box.

Darcy arrived just in time to hear, "Say hello to your grandmother for me. I know she loves double chocolate cream cakes."

Aha! He isn't homeless, thought Darcy. There's a grandmother somewhere. He hung back to scribble: *grandmother, double chocolate cream*. A good P.I. never overlooked seemingly minor details.

By the time he looked up, Tai was out of sight.

The alley was deserted. Not even an echoing footstep sounded on the broken pavement. Darcy wandered along the alley. Then suddenly, concealed between two walls, a tiny street appeared, with wooden fences lining each side. Darcy jumped up and peeped over some of the fences. Most yards were empty except for a few weedy shrubs and junk.

But visible in one, was the telltale flash of blue. Darcy quietly dragged a crate that was lying in the street to the fence. Carefully he climbed onto it and peeped over the fence.

13

He saw Tai sitting on steps at the base of a high staircase that led to the upper story, Darcy deduced, of what must be the main street stores. Tai wasn't saving any cake for his grandmother — he was hungrily stuffing mouthfuls of crumbs and cream into his mouth at a tremendous rate.

Needing time to think, Darcy ducked down and climbed off the crate.

The way Tai lived was strange. He seemed so hungry and scared. And where was the grandmother? Was she upstairs? Somehow, Darcy didn't think so. Just what was going on here?

Chapter Three
Under Surveillance

The next morning Darcy left home early, his backpack bulging with bread, milk, and apples. He made his way down the alley and into the lane.

He found Tai's fence and placed the bag of food by the gate, then sat down just around the corner to wait. Every few seconds he peeped into the lane.

Finally the gate swung outward and Darcy saw a hand reach out. The gate closed, and the bag of food was gone.

The next two mornings before school, Darcy left milk, bread, and canned food by Tai's gate. He only hoped his mom wouldn't notice the missing items.

On the third morning, he was just setting down the bag when the gate opened and Tai appeared beside him.

"You!" gasped Tai.

Guiltily, Darcy looked down at the ground, unsure of what to say. Finally he stammered, "Uh, hi. I thought maybe ... you were hungry."

The younger boy drew up his shoulders and the skittish colt look was back in his eyes.

Darcy quickly added, "It's okay. I haven't told anyone about you, Tai."

"How do you know my name?" asked Tai suspiciously.

"That's confidential information," Darcy replied. "But I can tell you my name. I'm Darcy."

Tai's shoulders relaxed slightly. "Hi, Darcy. Thanks for the food."

"No problem," said Darcy.

"Do you want to come in?" asked Tai.

Darcy checked his watch and nodded. "Well, maybe just for a minute." He told himself he should really go to school now, but this could be his chance to crack the case. And a good P.I. would never blow such an opportunity.

"I'd better go first," said Tai. "Be careful — the stairs are very steep. You'd better duck, too. You don't want to crack your head open!"

Darcy hesitated, but Tai had already crossed the yard to the crooked, wooden staircase. The rickety structure didn't look safe, but a good P.I. never ran in the face of danger.

"You coming?" called Tai.

"Yes, I'm coming," Darcy mumbled back.

At the landing, Tai disappeared through an outer door and Darcy slowly followed, stepping into dimness. A sharp click broke the silence and Darcy jumped as Tai snapped a bolt lock into place.

Now that was definitely suspicious. Darcy shivered and asked himself, why did Tai need to do that?

Chapter Four
The Missing Grandmother

Darcy squinted in the darkness. The old-fashioned kitchen was small but neat. There was no sign of the grandmother.

"Come and I'll show you something," said Tai.

Darcy followed him warily along a narrow hallway. Off to the side, a heavy wooden door stood bolted and padlocked.

Darcy's eyes widened and his heart thumped loudly. "W… What's in there?" he asked in a whisper.

"Oh, that," said Tai. "That's just the door to Costa's Barbershop downstairs. I'm only allowed to open that door if there's an emergency."

"What type of emergency?" asked Darcy, clenching his sweaty palms.

"I don't know," shrugged Tai. "Forget the door. Come and look." And he led the way under a low beam into a tiny living room.

Darcy noted that so far he had seen no television and no telephone.

Tai pulled back a curtain. "You can see the whole street from up here."

"Wow!" said Darcy. It was a perfect view. No one would even know they were being watched.

Tai spoke in a hushed voice. "Do you know that white van has been parked outside the Cribbs building for a couple of hours, every morning for three days. And the driver never gets out of the driver's seat. Very suspicious!"

Darcy looked at Tai with admiration. This kid was sharp.

"You know," said Tai. "I often saw you before I met you."

Darcy was about to reply when a sharp knock sounded on the outer door.

"Shh," hissed Tai. "Don't say anything and they'll go away."

The boys heard muffled voices out on the landing. "Where can he be?" "I hope he's okay." "He probably went to stay with friends."

Tai nudged Darcy and held his finger to his lips. Eventually whoever had been knocking gave up and left.

"Who was that?" asked Darcy, noticing Tai's pale face.

"I don't know," said Tai. "I never answer the door when Grandmother's not here."

So there was a grandmother. And she wasn't here. Judging by Tai's hunger, Darcy doubted if she'd been here for a while.

"Where is she?" he asked.

Tai looked fearful and he handed Darcy a crumpled note.

> Tai,
>
> I go to the hospital. Be back soon. Don't forget to keep door locked.
>
> Love, Grandmother

"That was six days ago," said Tai. "Grandmother hasn't come home."

Darcy gasped. "You mean you've been here on your own all this time? No wonder you were hungry!"

Tai rubbed the worn carpet with the toe of his shoe. "Grandmother must be very ill not to come home. But she will come back soon."

"Which hospital did she go to?" Darcy asked.

Pools of water flooded into Tai's dark eyes and his face crumpled. "That's the problem. I don't know. If anyone finds out I'm here alone, they might take me away. You can't tell anyone, Darcy. Anyone at all. Promise!"

Darcy grimaced. He knew they should tell someone. Maybe Mom could help them find Tai's grandmother.

"Twenty-four hours, Tai," Darcy said, hurrying toward the door. "I have to go now. Meet me at the gate tomorrow afternoon. If your grandmother's not here by then, I'll have to tell. Okay?"

Tai nodded, looking down at his feet.

Darcy wasn't sure he was doing the right thing by keeping Tai's secret. But he'd made a promise — and Darcy Devlin never broke a promise!

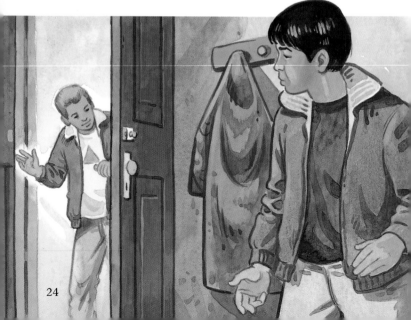

Chapter Five
Emergency!

The next morning, Darcy left another bag of food inside the gate.

The day dragged, and when the final bell rang, Darcy raced out of school toward the main street. The snowy curtain above Costa's Barbershop was closed, and Tai didn't meet him at the gate as they'd arranged. The food bag lay undisturbed.

Darcy's heart pounded with fear.

He hurriedly climbed the steps and knocked on the door. No answer.

Darcy remembered then that Tai never answered when his grandmother wasn't there. So he called, "Hey, Tai. It's me. Open the door." Still no answer! Perhaps Tai was scared that Darcy had told someone and that's why he wouldn't open the door.

After calling again, Darcy turned to walk back down the stairs when he heard a muffled cry from inside.

Anxiously, Darcy shook the door handle. It held tight. He heard the cry again, like someone was in great pain. He'd have to break in.

Darcy threw his weight against the door, but it refused to budge. He looked around frantically. The window! Beside the door was a small window, but what could he use to break it?

The crate! Darcy stumbled down the stairs, and in seconds returned with the crate. He gave a mighty lunge and slammed the crate into the glass, shutting his eyes as it shattered.

Carefully, he reached in past the jagged glass and unlocked the door. He stepped inside to hear a loud wail coming from somewhere down the hall.

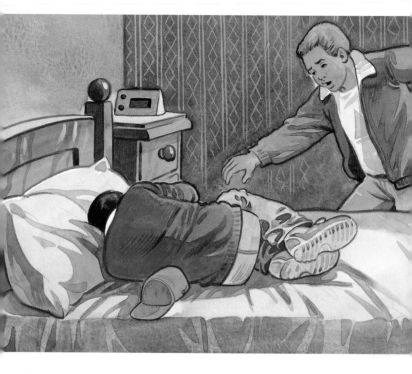

Darcy ran past the bolted door to a small room at the end of the hall. In the dimness he made out a moaning shape shaking on the bed.

"Tai, what's wrong?"

Tai drew his knees up to his chest and clutched his stomach, gasping with pain. He looked at Darcy with pleading eyes.

"What should I do?" asked Darcy.

Tai answered with a strangled moan.

Darcy ran back down the hall to the bolted door. He pushed the bolt, turned the key in the padlock, opened the door, and ran down the steep stairwell straight into a very surprised Costa.

"Where did you fall from? The sky?" Costa laughed. Then he saw Darcy's white face. "What's wrong?"

Within minutes of Costa's call, an ambulance from Western Hospital arrived. As Darcy's heart hammered in his chest, he watched Tai being carried out on a stretcher. "You'll be okay," he called to him.

Darcy watched the flashing lights disappear down the hill. "Please be all right," he whispered.

Darcy went back inside and had a long talk with Costa. He asked many questions.

Next he spoke to Tai's landlord. Darcy discovered Tai's grandmother's name and that Tai had no other family.

Then, with a little help from Mom, Darcy also spoke to the police and the local hospitals.

He asked many more questions and made lots of notes until finally, at the very same hospital that Tai had been taken to, he found Tai's missing grandmother.

He only hoped now that Tai would be all right.

Tai was fine — after his operation. Darcy visited Tai in the hospital and found out that Tai had to have his appendix removed. An old lady with snowy white hair sat beside the bed, and Tai shyly introduced his grandmother.

"So this is Tai's friend," she said, smiling. "Thank you for helping him. The hospital try to contact Tai. Is hard because we have no phone. They send someone to tell him, but he is good boy and never opens the door when I'm not there. Is mostly good thing, but not so good this time. Tai is lucky to have a friend like you. You must come visit when we come home."

31

"I will," said Darcy, with a grin. His detective agency could do with a partner, he thought. He could use some help investigating the white van that parked outside the Cribbs building every day. That guy had to be up to something, for sure ...